# TUNDRA

# TUNDRA

Donna Walsh Shepherd

A First Book

Franklin Watts
*A Division of Grolier Publishing*
New York  London  Hong Kong  Sydney
Danbury, Connecticut

For my favorite biologist and mountain climber,
my brother, Stan Walsh

Photo credits ©: Alaska Division of Tourism: 2 (Rex Melton), 36; Alaska Stock Images: 14, 26, 34 (all photos Johnny Johnson), 19, 32, 40 (all photos George Herben), 47 (Chris Arend), 51 (Clark Mishler), 54 (Al Grillo); Photo Researchers: 10, 24 (Bud Lehn-hausen), 29, 45 (both photos John Eastcott/YVA Momatiuk), 30 (Michael Giannechini), 38 (Tom McHugh), 56 (Jim Zipp); Scott T. Smith: cover, 3, 8, 52; Visuals Unlimited: 13 (C. P. Hickman), 21, 23, 49 (all photos Steve McCutcheon); Wildlife Collection: 42 (Henry Holdsworth).

Library of Congress Cataloging-in-Publication Data

Walsh Shepherd, Donna.
    Tundra / by Donna Walsh Shepherd.
        p.  cm. — (A First book)
    Includes bibliographical references and index.
    Summary: Examines the climate, land formations, plant life, and animals of the frozen arctic land called tundra, and discusses current preservation efforts.
    ISBN 0-531-20249-6 (lib. bdg.)  ISBN 0-531-15819-5 (pbk.)
    1. Tundra ecology—Juvenile literature.  2. Tundras—Juvenile literature.
    [1. Tundra ecology.  2. Tundras.  3. Ecology.]  I. Title II. Series.
    QH541.5.T8S45  1996
    574.5'2644—dc20          96-33777    CIP    AC

# CONTENTS

# Acknowledgments

Many thanks to all those who spoke with me about the tundra and reviewed this manuscript: the scientists from the Geophysical Institute at the University of Alaska in Fairbanks; the Roghairs from Barrow, Alaska—Jim, David, and Nick; biologist Stan Walsh; tundra engineer Jim Patterson; and my hiking friend, Mary Ellen Havens.

**Tundra is a land of tranquil beauty.**

# The Land
# of No Trees

The cold wind blows across the Arctic ice, over the seas and to the low, flat lands and the north mountains. It bends the Arctic cotton and grasses and flowers low to the ground. It ripples over lakes and marshes, pushing against the goose and loon nests. The bear and caribou turn their backs to the wind as they feed on berries and lichen. The fox and wolf trot through protected gullies looking for lemmings and ground squirrels feeding on the grasses and flowers. And the cold wind continues to blow across the silent, treeless land. This is the land of the Far North. This is the tundra.

In the northernmost regions of the northern continents and the high elevations of mountain ranges around the world, in the cold and nearly constant wind, a special

**An auroral display ripples through the
night sky above the ground, which is covered
with snow much of the year.**

environment has developed: the environment of the tundra. The word *tundra* comes from the Laplanders—the Sami native people of northern Scandinavia—and the Russians. It means "marshy plain" and "land of no trees." Canadians call this land the Barrens.

Even the harshest, most stark environments in the world often harbor beauty and abundant life. The tundra of the Far North is such a land. Perhaps nowhere in the world is life so hard as in this land of wind, extreme cold, and long winters. And few places in the world are as beautiful when the winter moonlight sparkles off the bluish-white snow and ice, the cold cracks the still air, and the brilliant auroras swirl overhead.

In early August, tundra nights become colder and the hours of darkness grow longer. Soon green plants turn red and gold, and then brown. They shed their precious seeds to the wind. Birds and their young gorge on these seeds and on water plants and insects as they prepare for the long trip south. Animals, from the smallest lemming to the largest grizzly bear, eat voraciously to store food energy for the long winter ahead.

In September, the marshes, lakes, and ground begin to freeze and the first snows come. For many months, the tundra will stay extremely cold. Even on the warmest days, the temperature will not rise above freezing. Snow will blow across the tundra for the next seven to nine months.

As the winter comes, many animals migrate to warmer places. Most birds fly far south. Other animals move to nearby protected mountain valleys. Of the animals that stay on the tundra, some hibernate, sleeping winter away, while others rest, conserve energy, and hunt for food only when they must.

Finally in the spring, the days gradually become longer and warmer. The snow begins to melt, and the river and lake ice begins to thaw. By June, the snow is mostly gone and the sun shines all night long. Plants sprout. Birds return and build nests. Other animals teach their young to hunt and gather food. Summer is the time to grow fat for the coming winter, to have young, and to spread seeds so that life may continue on the tundra.

Tundra covers more than 9 million square miles (23 million sq km) of the earth's surface. There are two types of tundra: Arctic tundra, which lies near the Arctic Ocean in the Far North, and Alpine tundra, which is found in high mountain areas from the Rocky Mountains to the Andes, from the Alps to the Himalayas.

Both kinds of tundra are formed by extreme cold and nearly constant wind. Cold and wind, and ground that may stay partially frozen all year, make it difficult for trees to grow and limit their size and number. Under such conditions, trees gradually disappear and are replaced by short bushes and shrubs. The point above which trees cannot grow is called the tree line and is the lower edge of the tundra. Of course, tundra is more than just tiny plants growing over a base of icy ground. It is the weather, the sun, the soils, and all the plants, animals, and people that live there. Together they make up the tundra ecosystem.

**Plant growth tapers off near the tree line.**

During the summer, when the sun shines all day and all night long, plants grow very fast and are very tender. They provide rich, easily digested food for all kinds of birds and other animals that inhabit the tundra, some as year-round residents, others as summer visitors.

**Though just a pup, this Arctic fox has already
learned to survive on the tundra.**

People also inhabit the tundra. Some make year-round homes; others come as visitors to see the beauty of the land. Some come to study and learn, others to take what riches they can.

Although we sometimes talk about the tundra as being fragile and easily destroyed, the people, animals, and plants of the tundra are hardy. They must be strong to live in such difficult conditions.

However, the balance between land, weather, plants, animals, and people is fragile. If the balance is disrupted, it can take centuries to repair itself. People must use great thought and care if they are to protect the delicate and beautiful tundra.

# Permafrost, Polygons, and Pingos

In the winter, the northernmost part of the earth, the North Pole, points away from the sun. Because of this tilt, the sun does not rise above the Arctic horizon for weeks. Dark, cold nights lead into dark, cold days. Winter temperatures can hover around -30°F (-34°C) for months.

During the summer, when the North Pole points toward the sun, the sun will not set below the horizon for weeks and shines twenty-four hours a day. Summer temperatures on the tundra swing wildly from day to day, even from hour to hour. Some days temperatures are close to 80°F (30°C), but most often they are nearer to 50°F (10°C). On the shortest day of winter, the place where the sun does not rise over the horizon and, on the longest day

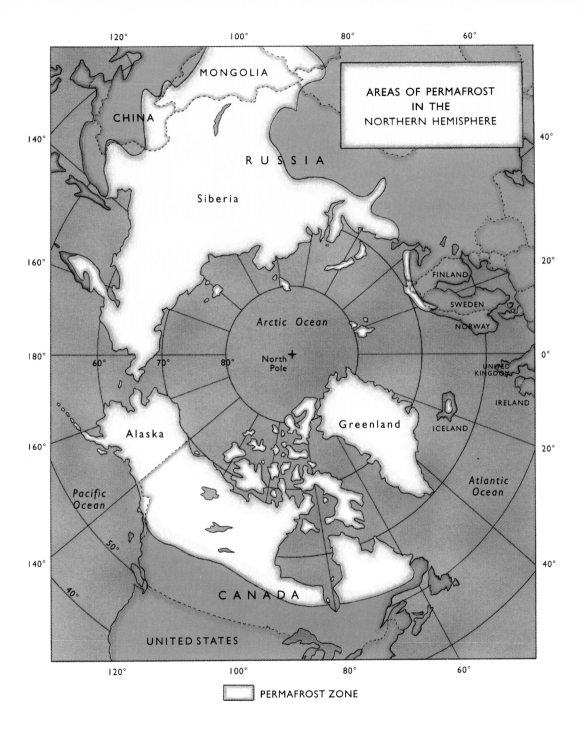

AREAS OF PERMAFROST
IN THE
NORTHERN HEMISPHERE

120°    100°    80°    60°

MONGOLIA

CHINA

140°                                                40°

R U S S I A

Siberia

160°                                                20°

FINLAND

SWEDEN

Arctic Ocean                                    NORWAY

180°    60°    70°    80°    North Pole                    0°

UNITED
KINGDOM

IRELAND

Alaska                    Greenland    ICELAND

160°                                                20°

Pacific
Ocean                                    Atlantic
Ocean

50°

140°                                                40°

40°

C A N A D A

UNITED STATES

120°    100°    80°    60°

PERMAFROST ZONE

of summer, the place where the sun does not set over the horizon is called the Arctic Circle.

During the long winters, the ground freezes deeply and solidly. When the short, cool summer finally arrives, even the long days of sun cannot undo the winter's effects. Only the top layer of frozen ground, the active layer, thaws during the summer and supports life. Beneath the active layer, a few feet down, the ground remains completely frozen season after season, year after year. This frozen ground is called permafrost. In the Far North, permafrost may extend more than 2,000 feet (610 m) into the ground.

About one-fifth of all the world's land lies atop permafrost. That includes all of Antarctica, 85 percent of Alaska, 50 percent of Canada, Russia, and the Baltic nations, 20 percent of China, and much of the high mountain areas around the world.

The tundra gets very little rain, usually between 5 and 9 inches (13 and 23 cm) a year. That is less than many of the world's deserts get. In most deserts, water evaporates quickly in the hot sun or sinks into the dry ground. On the tundra, however, only half of the rain and snowmelt evaporates or flows to the sea. The rest collects on top of the tundra, unable to sink into the ground because solid permafrost blocks the water from draining very far into the soil. Fortunately, the permafrost holds the precious water on the surface of the ground in thousands of marshes and lakes, where plants and animals can use it. Fresh water may appear abundant on the tundra, but it is a limited resource in this cold desert.

Water helps form other features on the tundra besides lakes and marshes. If you fly over the tundra, you will see that much of the lowland is cracked into giant polygon shapes that resemble the geometric pattern of a dried lake

**Polygons cracked into the earth are unmistakable features of tundra.**

bed. These many-sided shapes are so immense, you do not notice them from the ground.

The process that creates these polygons takes many, many years. In the summer, cold nights and warm days cause the land to contract and expand, opening long cracks, or fissures, across the tundra. Water seeps into these cracks, and the permafrost prevents it from draining away. When winter comes, that water freezes and expands. The soil and rocks frozen to this wedge of ice are forced out of the cracks and fissures to the ground surface with the expanding ice.

During the spring thaw, the ice wedge melts away and the soil and rocks frozen to it are left on the ground surface, creating a ridge or dam to catch next year's snowmelt. Year after year, snowmelt and rain seep into the cracks, freeze, and expand, forcing still more rocks and soil out of the ground and widening the fissures further. Some fissures are up to 10 feet (3 m) wide and 30 feet (9 m) deep. Eventually, these long fissures run into each other, creating a network of cracks in the land. It took hundreds of years for this giant honeycomb pattern to develop.

Sometimes lakes form in the depressions within the polygons. Other lakes are formed in natural low spots on the tundra. Thousands of these shallow lakes cover much of the tundra. In places where the wind blows consistently and forcefully over the lake surfaces, waves pound against the far shores, causing them to erode and collapse. These lakes becomes longer and longer, turning into blue ovals flowing in the direction of the wind.

When water trapped beneath the soil surface freezes
into ice wedges, it causes the land to buckle.

On the tundra, you will occasionally see round mounds called pingos. These mounds range from a few feet to more than 100 feet (30 m) high and can be more than 1,000 feet (305 m) across. Pingos look like something made by an ancient people, perhaps old graves or lookouts. In fact, they are not man-made, but they are, in a way, grave sites.

Pingos are made when water gets trapped between the permafrost and the ground surface. When there is not enough snowmelt or rain to renew the lakes, the lakes became clogged with grasses, soil, and debris. In winter, the old lake bed refreezes and the water left in it expands. In spring, the debris insulates it from thawing. Each spring more snowmelt runs into the base of the pingo and each winter that water freezes. As the years pass, the area that was once a lake grows into a high, round ice mound, marking the grave of a dead lake.

In marshy areas, something similar to the formation of pingos happens on a much smaller scale. Water may pool in small dips in the tundra. The water later freezes and expands, creating small rises in the land. Slowly, lumps about 1 foot (30 cm) high and across called tussocks form. Where tussocks polka-dot the tundra, walking can be difficult.

Ice and cold helped shape all of the tundra: the flat and rolling land, the ridges, the hills, and the valleys. Even the mountain ranges that edge the sea in places were

**Over time, large pingos have grown up near the
Mackenzie River, which flows through
Canada's Northwest Territories.**

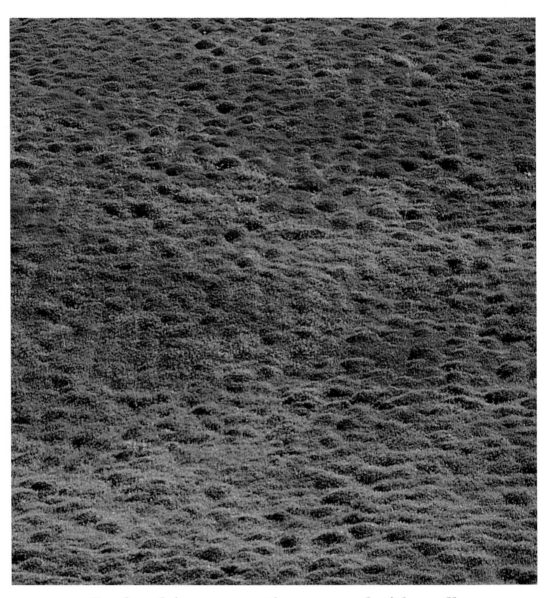

**Tundra plains are sometimes covered with small mounds of earth called tussocks.**

created with the help of long, deep cold and great sheets of ice. And as the ice and cold shape the land, they also shape the lives of the plants, the animals, and the people that live on the tundra.

**Low-bush cranberries, lichens, and
dwarf birch blanket autumn tundra.**

# Plants Above
# the Tree Line

Because wind and cold make it difficult for plants to grow, the farther north from the tree line you go, the smaller the plants become. As you travel north, leaving the great forest behind, you pass through bushes and shrubs about 6 feet (1.8 m) tall and small trees growing mostly in protected areas. Farther north, the bushes become shorter, only 3 feet (91 cm) high, and eventually knee high. Trees become few; even the few very old trees are short and thin. Finally, trees and bushes seem to disappear entirely. Miniature plants and trees only about 3 to 6 inches (8 to 15 cm) high form a thick, springy carpet underfoot.

On the cold, harsh tundra more than six hundred different types of plants grow. Lichens and mosses, grasses and sedges, and small plants and shrubs thrive here. Carpets of color spread uninterrupted across the tundra for miles: fields of yellow buttercups, acres of white Arctic cotton, vast sweeps of blue, pink, and purple wildflowers. Miniature willows and birches turn whole mountainsides green in the summer and red and gold in the fall. Berries grow thick most everywhere.

Lichen (pronounced *liken*) is one of the most common and hardiest tundra plants. This flat, rootless plant grows where other plants cannot, on rocks and bare ground. Lichen covers the tundra in splotches of orange, red, pale green, white, gray, and black. Although it is usually flat, some varieties grow wrinkles, small branches, or cups. Lichen plants range in size from less than ⅛ inch (3 mm) to nearly 10 feet (3 m) across. Lichen grows very slowly, but it lives for hundreds, even thousands, of years.

Lichen is actually two plants growing together: an alga and a fungus. The alga half of the plant manufactures food for both partners. The fungus half of the plant gathers and stores moisture for both plants and grows a hard, protective shell over the soft alga. The dependence of two living things on each other for survival like this is called symbiosis.

Moss, grasses, and sedges—a cousin of grasses—grow in areas too wet for lichen. The most common grass is Arctic cotton. The 1-foot- (30-cm-) high stems of Arctic cotton are topped with a cloud of white fluff. Long ago people living on the tundra used this soft cotton to line their boots and the tundra's spongy moss to line babies' diapers.

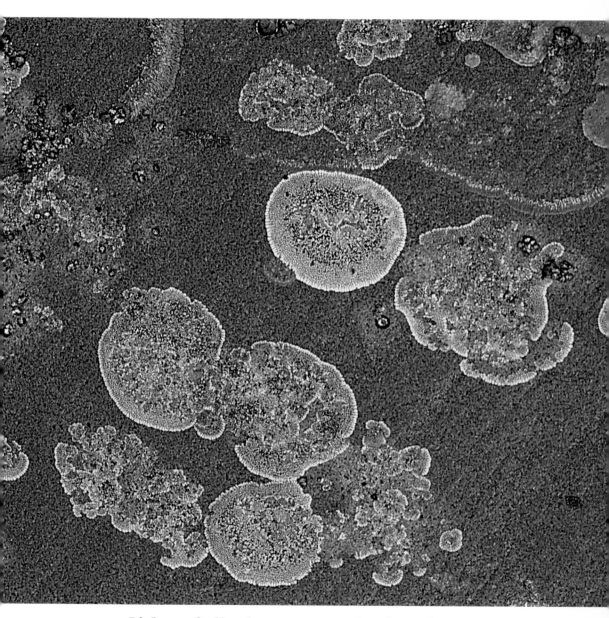

**Lichen of all colors grows on Arctic rocks.**

**Arctic cotton blows in an afternoon breeze.**

Perhaps some of the most beautiful plant life in the world are the colorful sweeps of delicate-looking flowering plants, trees, and shrubs that cover the face of the tundra. As fragile as these lovely plants appear, they have cleverly adapted to their environment by developing many special survival techniques.

Growing close to the ground protects tundra plants from the strong Arctic wind. Plants on the tundra often grow in tight mats. The ground beneath the matted plants usually stays much warmer than the air above the plants, which helps the roots to grow rapidly and seeds to form.

Because the tundra has qualities of a desert, many tundra plants have features common to desert plants. Some have hairy or waxy leaves that lose moisture slowly, and some store water for later use like a cactus does. Like desert plants, tundra plants are not typically tall. This reduces the surface area from which water can evaporate. And like desert plants, tundra plants must spread many seeds quickly during their short growing season. They must grow, flower, attract insects to pollinate them, and spread their seeds in only a few months.

Tundra plants often get a head start on the growing season by sprouting before the snow has completely melted. Most tundra plants are perennials; the same root stock grows a new plant each year. New plants also come from shoots sent out from parent plants.

In the summer, at blossoming time, the tundra is covered with great fields of beautiful flowers. Masses of reds, yellows, purples, blues, pinks, and whites spread as far as you

**Inside an Arctic poppy flower, sticky
pollen grains are ready for distribution.**

can see. These flowers are more than pretty; they are practi-
cal. Rich colors attract insects. Inside the flower, the insects
rub against the plant's pollen, spreading the reproductive
material within the plant and to other plants. This process,
which allows plants to reproduce, is called pollination.

Besides color, plants use other techniques to attract insects. Bell-shaped flowers offer insects protection from the wind. Other plants, like the yellow buttercup and Arctic poppy, have a rotating cup-shaped flower that follows the sun, gathering solar heat. The center of these flowers can be much warmer than the outside air and offers insects a welcome retreat from the Arctic cold. Some flowers have special patterns to attract insects. White flowers might have thin red lines from the edge of the petal to the center of the flower to guide flying insects, much the way runway lights guide planes to the airport.

The colorful blanket of plants on the tundra is far more than a beautiful sight. That layer of plant life insulates and shields the underground permafrost from the sun and warm air that could melt it and cause the ground to collapse into a mush that could not support plant or animal life. Because the tundra plants grow so fast in the sun, which shines twenty-four hours a day, they are very tender and nutritious. They make excellent food for the many tundra animals that depend on the plants for survival.

**Arctic fox kits huddle together near their den.**

# A World Full
# of Wildlife

The stark land of the tundra is not nearly as empty as it seems. The tundra is home to billions of insects and millions of birds. It is home to lemmings, ground squirrels, and Arctic hares, to foxes and wolves, to musk oxen and caribou, and to barren-ground grizzly bears. Pike, Arctic char, trout, and other fish populate the lakes. And seals, walruses, and polar bears live along the Arctic Ocean shore.

Insects are the most populous inhabitants of the tundra, and among the most important. Mosquitoes and black flies are a plentiful food source for all kinds of birds. Insects also help seeds mature and ripen by spreading pollen from plant to plant. The seeds provide a food source for animals both small and large and grow into new plants.

**Birds fill the tundra sky in early spring and fall.**

Each spring, even before the first plants send tender shoots through the snow, even before the first insect larvae hatch, birds begin flying north. Arctic terns come from Antarctica and plovers come from South America. The flyways (the air routes of migrating birds) all over North America are full of ducks, geese, loons, and swans making their way back north. More than one hundred species of birds spend the summer feasting on rich tundra plants, insects, and fish. They nest, have their young, and then begin the long flight back to their winter homes. And the next year, they will return. This travel back and forth is called migration.

Not all birds migrate. Some birds, like ravens and gulls, winter on the tundra. The ptarmigan, whose brown summer feathers turn white in the winter, and the snowy owl, which remains white all year long, also stay on the tundra come winter.

Lemmings, a cousin of the field mouse, live in tunnels under the mat of vegetation or snow. All winter long, they feed on withered plants and stored seeds. Weasels, ermines, foxes, and wolves dig into snowdrifts looking for lemming tunnels and follow the tunnels to the lemmings' nests. Owls fly overhead, looking for places where drifting snow has uncovered lemming tunnels.

Lemmings breed very quickly and have many broods in a season. In years when the tundra is thick with lemming colonies, the animals that feed on lemmings grow fat and healthy. When the tundra is too thick with lemmings, something odd happens. The lemmings gather in

**Lemmings are known for their
unusual mass migrations.**

groups and begin running across the tundra looking for new homes. More lemmings join them. Masses of lemmings, masses of tiny feet running together, head north. They do not stop to eat; they do not stop at all. When they come to great rivers, they swim across. When they come to hills or mountains, they climb over. When they finally reach the Arctic Ocean, they plunge in, ready to swim across. But the ocean is too great, and masses of lemmings drown. Lemming tunnels throughout the tundra are left nearly empty. In a few years, however, the remaining lemmings will have enough offspring to make the tundra thick with lemmings again. And once again, the massive race to the sea will begin.

When the lemming population is low, the foxes, wolves, and owls that prey on lemmings will have hard times. Winter food will be scarce and they will have fewer offspring.

Not all large tundra animals prey on other animals. Musk oxen eat grasses and plants. The sturdy musk ox resembles a small buffalo, but it is related to the goat. Protected by their thick coats, these woolly animals stay out on the tundra plains foraging for food all winter. Their soft undercoat, called qiviut, is considered finer than cashmere. In the spring, Alaskan Native women from local villages gather this wool and knit prized scarves and garments to sell.

Caribou also feed on plants. In the summer, caribou live in small groups across the tundra, eating lichen and grasses and giving birth to their young. They are always on the move: eating, shaking off bothersome insects, searching for new and better feeding grounds, or migrating long distances. It is said that caribou take three steps for every bite of food they eat, so that food must be highly nutritious to keep them going. In the fall, the small groups gather together, and then the larger groups gather.

**Musk oxen crowd together for protection
from the Arctic wind.**

Finally, in herds of thousands, the caribou move across the tundra and through the mountain passes to the inland forest valleys for the winter.

Caribou keep warm all winter because their thick coat is made of hollow hairs that trap warm air close to their bodies. During the winter the caribou dig through the snow to find lichen and grasses. Their wide hooves, which act like snowshoes to keep them on the surface of snowy or marshy ground, also make good shovels. The word *caribou* comes from a North American Indian word for "shoveler." Caribou and reindeer are actually the same animal. Reindeer, however, are domesticated, raised for their meat and milk.

Tundra wolves travel closely with the caribou herds. They live in families of five to fifteen animals called packs. Each pack is led by an alpha, or lead, male and female. The alpha pair will produce a litter of four to eight pups each year, and all the family members take care of the pups. Wolves are very sociable and caring for each other, but they are wary of humans.

Tundra wolves kill only for food. Although caribou is their favorite meal, wolves also eat mice, lemmings, rabbits, weasels, even berries. After a kill, a wolf stores partially digested meat in its stomach to take back to the pups or the nursing mother. The pups greet the hunter wolf with affection and licks on the mouth. The hunter then spits up the partially digested meat for the young to eat.

It is not uncommon to see a wolf walk right through a caribou herd without disturbing it. Caribou know they

**A grizzly bear lunges effortlessly for dinner.**

can outrun wolves. Wolves can catch only caribou that are very young or those that are old, ill, or weak. To catch a caribou, wolves hunt together and one wolf tricks the caribou into running toward the other wolves. Each pack travels in a territory covering about 200 square miles (518 sq km). They follow the caribou out onto the tundra in the spring and back to the protected valleys in the winter. Wolves live above ground year round, except for the alpha female, who digs a den into a sandy hillside to have her pups.

The ruler of the tundra is probably the barren-ground grizzly bear, one of the fastest land animals alive. These bears eat both plants and animals. Because the inland grizzly eats mostly berries, it is much smaller than its south coastal plains relatives, which eat mostly high-protein salmon. During the fall, grizzlies move south to dens in the warmer hills and mountains to hibernate and give birth to the next generation of tundra rulers.

# Living on
# the Tundra

Ten thousand years ago, people crossed to America from Asia and turned to the North to find homes. Like the Sami in Lapland and others in Russia, they made their home on the tundra at the edge of the Arctic Ocean. Surviving in such extreme cold took creativity and determination. It was often a difficult existence.

The people of the tundra were one of the few cultures in history that could not depend on grains, rice, or roots. They were hunters and gatherers who wasted nothing. From a seal, for example, they took its oil for heat and lamplight, its skin for clothing, boats, and shelters, its bones for tools, and its meat for food.

Because they lived so closely with animals, the people of the tundra honored the animal's spirit. They always

**Like his ancestors before him,
an Inuit boy fishes with a spear for Arctic char.**

returned some bones of a harvested animal to the sea so that the spirit of the animal could return home. They always thanked the animal for giving its life so that the people might survive.

Today tundra villages rely on many modern conveniences. Heavily insulated wood homes have replaced houses of driftwood, animal skins, and earth. The sounds of satellite phones, television, and radio break the winter silence. Canned and boxed food barged in during the summer supplement birds, fish, and seal, whale, and caribou meat. Baby diapers come from boxes instead of marshes. And dogsleds are parked alongside snowmobiles, cars, trucks, and airplanes. In spite of all these modern conveniences, the cold still shapes life on the tundra. It is still a difficult existence that requires creativity and determination.

Some people wonder how anyone can possibly live on the tundra in the winter and why anyone would want to. They forget that when a place is home you overlook inconveniences like cold and darkness. Longtime tundra dwellers consider winter normal and comfortable. To them, summer is the odd season. Tundra residents get used to the cold. In subzero weather, when visitors bundle in heavy layers, tundra children play tag outside in shirtsleeves.

People on the tundra do prepare for cold, however. They build well-insulated houses. They often own more coats than pairs of jeans. If they drive to the store or to a meeting in the winter, they leave their vehicles running

**Winter on the tundra is often dark and always cold.**

while they are inside. The engine will be difficult to restart once it is turned off.

During the tundra winter, the darkness is not as total as it might seem. When the sun disappears for weeks at a time, it circles just below the horizon. Long periods of dusk light each day give way to a night of moonlight reflecting off the snow. A midwinter night in California can seem much darker than the same winter night in Barrow, Alaska. In the summer, the sun circles just above the horizon all day and all night. In the early fall and late spring, the sun rises and sets in the north, giving more long days of light. In the late fall and early spring, the sun rises and sets in the south.

In very cold weather on the tundra, houses are surrounded by a glowing cloud, almost like an aura. This habitation fog is caused by moisture and heat escaping from the house and vaporizing, much as a person's breath does in cold weather. When sunlight hits this fog, ice particles catch the light and, like prisms, break it into tiny rainbows. The very air sparkles with "diamond dust."

The most difficult aspect of living on the tundra is building on permafrost. If the insulation layer of plants and soil is removed, or the ground becomes heated, the permafrost may melt and collapse. Each year the melted area will grow larger and soon fail to support buildings, roads, and water pipes. On the tundra, buildings are erected on stilts to allow heat to escape upward instead of being absorbed into the ground and melting the permafrost.

Things many people take for granted, like running water and indoor plumbing, are difficult and expensive to provide on the tundra. Because pipes running through frozen ground may freeze or may melt the ground, many plumbing systems run above ground, on 2-foot- (60-cm-) high pilings or in troughs. Both aboveground and underground pipes must be insulated at least to three times the

**Houses and pipes built on permafrost soils
are raised to prevent heat from melting the
permafrost and causing the ground to collapse.**

diameter of the pipe. In some plumbing systems the water is constantly circulated through the pipes just to keep it from freezing. Other systems run by vacuum.

In some larger communities, ground work like building, laying pipes, and burying the dead is often done in the winter. In the summer, soggy ground can collapse onto a work project. Workers use giant chain saws to cut the frozen tundra into blocks, which they remove. They then complete the underground work and replace the blocks of frozen ground. Before chain saws came to the tundra, the dead were stored in a special building until spring, when graves were dug and a community funeral held.

Even today, many settlements have no piped-in water or plumbing. Water is trucked or carried to homes and businesses and stored in large tanks. Human waste is kept in containers called honey buckets and transported to sanitation dumps in tankers called honey wagons.

Food, heating, and gas are also expensive on the tundra. The oil mined close to many tundra communities is shipped far away for processing and then shipped back. Most food is shipped in, and prices are high. A gallon of milk that may cost two dollars in Seattle can cost ten dollars on the tundra. A five-dollar hamburger can cost fifteen dollars. Fresh fruits and vegetables are scarce, usually of poor quality, and costly. Tundra residents who travel often return home with fruit and vegetables in their luggage.

In spite of the difficulties, most people enjoy the sense of community they find living on the tundra. Although they are far from the main areas of population,

**Tundra dwellers play with a
homemade sled on a sunny afternoon.**

there is little feeling of isolation. No one is lost or forgotten here as they might be in large cities. Everyone knows and takes care of everyone else. Tundra dwellers have a real understanding of where they live in the world and of being part of nature's community.

**51**

**Early tundra dwellers considered this
varied land of mountain peaks, shallow ponds,
and colorful vegetation sacred.**

# A Sacred Place?

The early tundra dwellers believed that land was sacred. They believed that if you took care of the land, it would take care of you. Looking out over the tundra lakes and marshes reflecting the Arctic sky, or over the flowered plains to the jagged mountains lining the horizon, one wonders if perhaps this land is sacred for its beauty alone.

Underneath the beauty, the tundra hides a wealth of minerals: oil, natural gas, coal, even gold. Currently, a battle is being waged over the fate of the tundra. Some people point to a need for the massive energy sources frozen in the permafrost, and the jobs and money those resources would provide. Others warn of the catastrophic damage that even small wounds to the tundra can do. Tundra takes a long time to heal, much longer than other envi-

**Workers attempt to clean up the worst oil spill in U.S. history, which occurred after the oil tanker *Exxon Valdez* hit an Alaskan reef.**

ronments. Caterpillar tracks made during World War II destroyed tundra vegetation that insulated frozen ground from the sun. Those areas of melting permafrost have grown steadily larger and deeper. The scars are now lakes.

Already areas of the tundra are polluted. Refuse from development, mining, travelers, and exploration litters the tundra. Air pollution and acid rain come in on the winds from central Europe and Russia. Oil spills have destroyed plant and animal habitats. The risks of development are a concern to all.

New and safer methods of exploration are continually being developed. Tundra vehicles now travel on giant balloon tires, which put less pressure on the tundra than a human footstep. Garbage, from loose paper to old machinery, is removed and recycled. Still, to develop the tundra further, we must gain more knowledge about how to care for the land and how to prevent leaving destructive marks upon it.

Scientists are continually searching for secrets of the tundra. Some study the survival techniques of tundra plants and animals. Others examine the village remains of the first Arctic people to learn how they lived. Others excavate animal remains, like the fossilized dinosaur remains in the Colville River Valley, where bones of eight different species have been found. Still others study the ice and world weather patterns. Because the temperatures of the upper levels of the ancient permafrost are rising significantly, they believe that permafrost is a reliable indicator of global warming.

The tundra has much to teach us. Perhaps more important, we need to learn to appreciate the call of the loon and the sight of wildflowers bowing in the wind. Perhaps we need to watch the caribou walk the mountain crest, the grizzly graze on hillside berries, and the sun circle the sky without setting. If we stand in the ankle-deep wilderness, facing the wind, we will know we are part of this land, caretakers of this land—this silent, windswept, top-of-the-world land called tundra.

# For Further Reading

Barrett, Ian. *Tundra and People*. Morristown, N.J.: Silver Burdett, 1982.

Carr, Terry. *Spill: The Story of the Exxon Valdez*. New York: Franklin Watts, 1991.

George, Jean Craighead. *One Day in the Alpine Tundra*. New York: Crowell, 1984.

Hiscock, Bruce. *Tundra: The Arctic Land*. New York: Atheneum, 1986.

Mowat, Farley. *Never Cry Wolf*. Boston: Little, Brown, 1963.

Murie, Margaret E. *Two in the Far North*. New York: Knopf, 1962.

Osborn, Kevin. *The Peoples of the Arctic*. New York: Chelsea House, 1990.

Sayre, April P. *Tundra*. New York: 21st Century Books, 1994.

Silver, Donald M. *One Small Square: Arctic Tundra*. New York: W. H. Freeman, 1994.

Williams, Terry Tempest, and Ted Major. *The Secret Language of Snow*. San Francisco: Sierra Club, 1984.

*Related Fiction*

George, Julie Craighead. *Julie of the Wolves*. New York: HarperCollins, 1972.

Houston, James. *Frozen Fire: A Tale of Courage*. New York: Macmillan, 1977.

London, Jack. *Jack London's Stories of the North*. New York: Scholastic, 1989.

Mowat, Farley. *Lost in the Barrens*. Boston: Little, Brown, 1956.

# INDEX

*Italicized* page numbers indicate illustrations.

# About the Author

Donna Walsh Shepherd lives with her husband and three sons in Anchorage, Alaska. She teaches literature and writing at the University of Alaska. During the summer, when she is trying to keep moose out of her garden, Ms. Walsh Shepherd likes to hike in the Alaskan bush and travel to foreign countries.